D0758361

The Year of Our Birth

THE YEAR OF
OUR BIRTH

SANDRA
McPHERSON

THE ECCO PRESS / NEW YORK

First published by The Ecco Press in 1978

1 West 30th Street, New York, N.Y. 10001

Published simultaneously in Canada by

Penguin Books Canada Limited

Printed in the United States of America

The Ecco Press logo by Ahmed Yacoubi

Typography by Cynthia Krupat

The publication of this book is partially supported by

a grant from The National Endowment for the Arts.

Grateful acknowledgment is made to the following publica-
tions in which these poems first appeared: *American Review:*
"Gnawing the Breast," *Antaeus:* "Children," "On a Picture
of My Parents Together in the Second Grade," "On Coming
Out of Nowhere," "Orange Peels," "The Compound Eye."
Esquire: "Cellar Spiders." *Field:* "A Coconut for Katerina,"
"An Anonymous Pornographic Valentine," "Senility," "The
Bittern," "The Mouse," "To an Alcoholic." *Harper's:* "For
Fathers," "The Gun Is Such a Horse," "Wearing White." *The
Iowa Review:* "Centerfold Reflected in a Jet Window," "1943."
Ironwood: "Childish Landscape," "January Apples." *The Ohio
Review:* "Solvents." *Poetry:* "Extract," "In a Garden," "Letter
After the Poems of a Friend," "Poem Whose First Stanza Is
Martin Heidegger on Georg Trakl," "Sentience," "Studies in
the Imaginary," "The Heredity of Systems," "Triolet."

Library of Congress Cataloging in Publication Data

McPherson, Sandra. / The year of our birth.

(American poetry series; 15) / I. Title.

PS3563.A326Y4   811'.5'4   77-85295

ISBN 0-912-94648-2 (*hardbound*)

ISBN 0-912-94649-0 (*paperback*)

for Phoebe

I am thankful for a grant from

the National Endowment for the Arts

which enabled me to work on many of

these poems in 1974 and 1975.

And grateful for a Guggenheim fellowship

that helped the book to completion

in 1976 and 1977.

Contents

The Year of Our Birth

1943

I was born the year of the gray pennies.
They'll find me in another layer, the skull
above the deviating Lincoln heads

worth ten or fifteen cents by now.
The smile won't be in the bone,
so they will think that I've depreciated.

But that money didn't last. Gray did
and camouflaged our war,
woodchucks, catbirds—

the year of our birth sank beneath us.
The bank was rock.
On top of me are falling all the saved.

For Fathers

The closest we came
was doing the thousand-
piece puzzle.
Wasting time
on that painting of the tower

was not as wasteful as some years
(were they building it
or could all those characters
be bellringers,
red-bloused, grain-

trousered and humbly
enough all men).
Except at the time
it's painted
the picture matters

less than our own people.
His children
interrupt the painter.
Forgiveness almost becomes
an impatient habit. "Paint

me a little picture!"
begs the son
and ever since
the inch by inch response
has hung in the home

the ruby-
throated hummingbird
hangs outside—
oh the iridescent fragments
and the fathers.

Extract

—Here I am like Jacob,
fallen from the ladder
that holds finally this angelic roofer—
and suddenly the only thing real to me
is that vine of grapes.
I saw you kissing bruises
such as little girls complain of
whom you'd lift clear off the ground
to dance.

When I was a child and left alone
I had a funny way of using my eyes:
I saw the nearest flowers
as if they were twice their distance.
And these small suns were untouchable
and traveling,
traveling away.

And then it would be Sunday,
day of things withheld.
I'd stand below the church doors
and it is they, I think, I liked most
in religion—
immense doors and my vacillation
between the balcony inside
and flights of birds.

Great spaces, I'm thinking of for you,
as you seem to ask,
vast intervals.

Childish Landscape

Where the crickets scratched by the oak
a hill watched stars come out.
Estrella, Sterne

said our old people,
hair lifting and stirring.

The valley's other rim
was fatherly, darker,
submerged like the breath of their god.

On that dark rim
they said the children looked
as brown as quail.

But we were really blue inside
like the small triangle of ocean
having its own sunset

after theirs.
This is the proof of God, they said.
The present. Because you see.

The Heredity of Systems

They were always telling us
the importance of love
and how there is an animal in it
not as tender as a deer
not noble as a bear
maybe low like a badger
or hot like red fox fur
and how it has this single mistake
like a child who can't learn numbers
modeling his pages
with love of their shapes
That's what they said
for generations
until we could no longer remember
being born
nor get up and run
on our first red feet
to escape the people who loved us
When we could we began showing them
how it is paramount
the smoke in bacon
how it is human supernatural and animal
because it is the birthplace
of likeness
and the embodiment
of reasoning

On a Picture of My Parents Together in the Second Grade

Dust as beige pongee,
'cot blossoms inside the margins,
the palms with thin tigerstripes of blood and gravel . . .

But today, without a license, as I drive
a car black as the blind mules
in the old McPherson cinnabar mine,

it's for some foolish emergency
that I crash into the schoolyard,
into the fence that worried over everyone

both our generations knew.
This is the last time for me.
I will never go anywhere so quickly as into the past.

I wait but no one comes to help or accuse.
The square is full of devils
winding all free dust up into themselves. The accident

has spared each brick, electric bell, cursive letter, girl
in hula skirt and principal behind
the bricks, daydream

of lilac scent, violet
of iodine.
Anyone I might have hit,

their intelligence ordered here from madness of their parents'
bed to sit by surname and stand by height,
still belongs to tomorrow,

to the very green soap, salamander tank, and
zither which have always kept them wise
and curious.

A little mixing on the fingertips and my blood forms brothers,
the dust spins over the crosswalk,
I slam the door and follow the cloud home.

They will be glad I too am still together.

Poem Whose First Stanza Is Martin Heidegger on Georg Trakl

The morning too has its twilight.
The day rising in twilight,
evening then is also a rising.
Clarity sheltered in the dark is blueness.
Like a boat that does not reach
the pond's surface
the dead do not rise.
Their pain is appeased,
they lie in a silver grove,
the pallor of death, the sparkle
of the stars. The soul apart
softly wanders
    in the landscape.
If all but landscape shakes in modesty,
inglorious, the human condition
light as air
forgotten against the cliffs,
and trouble glints
off sides of scattered rock,
all together the world,
our modest bodies,
is not modest.
Passage of the sun still favors
the whole object
and what is wrong with our place
for that soul?

It is not so fine a thing
it should abandon
like worn odorous slippers
what we have not misused
but only overworked—
our bodies like sympathy notes
and friends helping us move.
Who wants to go wandering in space
with no peculiarities but sweep,
clarity, and the beginnings of air?
   As I grew up
my street became less wide,
the trees immature,
the walks littered
with too few pepperberries and palm fronds.
Crowds jostle
on the once bare walk to the belltower.
Music can no longer be heard
in its old wooden building
where everything listened,
the ivy, the auditorium door.
My dreams in happy childhood
were nightmares.
I abandoned myself
to them. Waking up,
to start over profanes the original beginning.
   Except there is a twilight zone
where I bend back, continue

my past
when the sun and young stories
rose and illumined and set
and ran time well.
In one of the stories
a white road bobbed over low hills
and leaned up in the distance
so that the early days seem
in rural sunshine
like an afterlife.
    Each newer life too
accounts for itself by a few prospects.
Rain, fleabane, hay, seiner,
the newest turning into the family farm.
The sheep rise up and follow the sun;
the mists rise.
Here is the white road—
ridiculous,
it makes me feel like a child.
    Here I am then
in the only life that is clear,
clearer than all that's said about it
and less lucid than
the blank evening sky
on which any silhouette is shelter,
wealth without gain,
the mass of a pitched roof
or the new leaves,

black and tender
self-extremes
on the evening.

For Early in Marriage

1

You don't remember me
as I was in those days
when you thought of no one else.
You remember the landlady

who trusted you and let
you fall behind; and I the night
a friend enthralled you with a lie
he had six months to live.

But I can't remember knowing you at all,
just listening to you study
from the bed and learning what the examiners
would force you to recall.

2

Lay down your study of ambiguities
and as the nurse brings in the baby
tell me what it was like last night
not sleeping with me.

"I saw the stems of words
cut, and the nonce created lonely,
I thought of calling out
the baby's full ignorance and scream—"

—She must have thoughts in dreams,
but when awake she thinks aloud
in the coarsest and most chaste language for
Open your blouse.

Children

She will run to you for love whoever
you are, you who'd forgotten what you look like.
She keeps a book of forms in her arms,
like a fitter exact on waists.

And perhaps I'll have to pull her from
celebrating her birth between your legs
although she is my only child
and good at it and best of all the children

you don't have. You know her face
can't be yours. But let me become a stranger,
not act myself, beat on the mirror and cry—
she sees I look like her alone.

And sticking her face in mine, smearing my
lipstick with her index finger, igniting
the pale mustache, drawing the seeing mirror
of her glasses down oil

on my cheeks, she hangs my picture
forever in her head. So that she always
sees to me when I am down
and thinks the way to raise me is

to climb aboard me toe for toe, palm
lidding palm so I can't withdraw
or go out of our single mind
to have another child.

A Coconut for Katerina

Inside the coconut is Katerina's baby. The coconut's hair, like
Katerina's brown hair.
Like an auctioneer Katerina holds the coconut, Katerina in her
dark fur coat
covering winter's baby, feet in the snow. Katerina's baby is the
milk
and will not be drinking it.

Ropes hanging down from the trees—are they well ropes? Ropes
on a moss
wall. Not to ring bells but used for climbing up and down
or pulling, I mean bringing. Anchor ropes on which succulent ropy
seaplants grow.

And floating like a bucket of oak or like a light wooden dory,
the coconut bobs,
creaking slowly, like a piling or a telephone pole with wet wires
downed by a thunderstorm over its face.

This baby's head, this dog's head, this dangerous acorn is the
grocer
of a sky-borne grocery store where the white-aproned grocer or
doctor imprints it
with three shady fingerprints, three flat abysses the ropes will
not cross.

What of it? There is enough business for tightrope walkers in
this jungle.
The colonizers make a clearing

for a three-cornered complex of gas stations, lit with a milky
    spotlight
at night.

                        And here we dedicate this coconut to Katerina. We
    put our hand
on the round stomach of Katerina. We put our five short ropes
    of fingers on the lost
baby of Katerina and haul it in to the light of day and wash
    it with sand.

Coconut, you reverse of the eye, the brown iris in white, the
    white center
in brown sees so differently. The exposed fibrous iris,
the sphere on which memory or recognizing must have latitude
    and longitude
to be moored

or preserved in the big sky, the sea's tug of war. The tugging of
    water
held in and not clear. Lappings and gurglings of living hollows
    half filled,
half with room
for more empty and hopeful boats and their sails.

On Coming Out of Nowhere

In the tropics my father drove us for the belladonna
—immune until the rest of us grew well—
and we did not hallucinate the purple
crabs sideways across the beach road in the lightning . . .

Your aquarium and the snow rising
are enough to make me tell you this,
the adoption I knew nothing of
but that I want it again and again,

while around your door the new snow makes it hard
to come and go. This is half your home.
Soon the darkened doorway will admit your wife,
the red light of her hair, as if from nowhere.

Gnawing the Breast

of a fallen sparrow, the prairie dog first softens
it with his teeth then frees and finishes the piece,
    his head high.
    The she-dog eats stems of grass.
Meat-eater tries to make love to grass-eater.
But no, she'd rather lie almost flat as water,
    contracting and rolling while she sleeps.

Young girls keep running up and asking me if she
    is dying.
She sleeps, smaller and darker of the two.
They attribute despair inside her to her shade and size.
    She might also be old-fashioned,
    a baby could kill her.
And then, inclusive kids, they nose about what I am

doing; why I am doing it; what I do when I'm not
    doing this;
till one squeals that she hates what I do because
    it puts her to sleep.
When they run off kicking, the prairie dog wakes
and otters through the grass: while I think,
    Pretty things, when will you have earned

your beauty sleep? And when have eaten enough love
    to live on love
though you throw so much away? Well, it's just a tiny
guilty zoo. The keeper wishes he could feed
    the animals more blossoms.

I ask him, "Where did you get that hill that wasn't
        there before?"

"A new grave," he says.
Maybe it was Aesop, diving, doing research as a
universal bird and ending up in the mouth of this dog.
    The hill will give it a viewpoint.
I think if I could climb that hill,
the air would be cooler, fresher, as it always used to be
    on ones I didn't know the source of.

And the hill might even move a little, feeling the kick
        of a child.

Cellar Spiders

Before he died Rawson wrote
verses to his old wife
and sewed them together on paper
the color of whirring pholcus spiders
The dust that collected
was enough to make a man

That's what it means to me too
That's why there are no mistakes in poetry

To an Alcoholic

I make you sightsee the sheer walls,
The rapids, hanging over them
A ledge of hand-high cactus with a
Bourbon cup.

That's how I keep you sober
As a cony's bed. You get yourself
Drunk. You're in torn hands that wish
To be in good.

There is no blood in the golden flower.
The tuns grow shoved together
Storing up their leap. The country's dry
But snowmelt

Sends the river high. "Up there,"
You say, "a spring's a waitress,
Long legs underground from me"
And "Hardest

Thing on the face of God's earth
To get a glass of whiskey."
I know they're prickly,
Those dry-side

Visions. We need some glory
Always. These know only cache and wait.
Their time is right: to each his own
Piss-golden light.

In a Garden

I'd just as soon be a skull, among elements that love
my elements, as teach the thick-skinned and the faint to seize
life. They should teach me. Everything out of doors knows
what's good for it, a wordless book on how and when
to eat and what to sniff at. All compete to bathe,
dive, hover over, splash each other

and grow so clean they drink what made some other
species clean. In troops of six the yellow warblers love
to ambush puffy robins who increase as they bathe,
roughing themselves up. The warblers seize
a spot over robins' heads and beat as when
a flag proclaims an untenable mountain. Who knows

how a lightweight, free from human scales, knows
he's frightening? If I'm for the small, in other
words, neglectable, and I know something big when
I see it, I'll go a little further. Even say I love
what complicates, compensates for me, can seize
the imagination, overturn the waters with oxygen, bathe

us in historical light. What makes so many bathe
at once—hour, air, cocked eye of the light? One knows
and all the others know. Brown, spotted, bright, they seize
the muddy ground around the pool. Each from the other
wants the chance that comes to all—to love
himself with coolness, shallow water, and get out when

clean. A gorgeous blue obstacle, the jay comes just when
the least are taking turns. They will bathe
him with insults he, the grossest cheat, must love
or not be himself without their jeers, envy, and (one knows)
very real longing. It's a day like other
days, peace levels in me like water, and other lives seize

that very slack to trouble. Get hold of yourself!—seize
the difference between these angels and your friends; when
you've matched them, let them love one another.
That unifies the world. Then wash your hands; bathe;
steam; know what every species knows
that tries, at least once in a while, to love.

Now it is the other half of day. Who'll bathe
at night, join (not seize) the small lonely pool when
no one else knows? Will we sleep through its love?

Triolet

She was in love with the same danger
everybody is. Dangerous
as it is to love a stranger,
she was in love. With that same danger
an adulteress risks a husband's anger.
Stealthily death enters a house:
she was in love with that danger.
Everybody is dangerous.

An Anonymous
Pornographic Valentine

("You were expecting something a little more sentimental perhaps?")

The Stanford linear accelerator trembles from a man's jealous
    race
to the mailbox. He's sending me, inside the white homemade
sarong of this valentine, his best rough draft.

He's unrevised, uncircumcised. So! I am a thought in the mind
of the Unknown Soldier. An old salt? Or is this a taste of his
    love
that he's memorialized shaker in hand in this photo quickly
    shot?

How I feel for Saint Valentine, who delivers me this day
a last, a first, uncensored heart. Only a man could imagine
    Lot's wife
turning into a pillar of salt. She a memorial to him. For
    valentine

I was expecting the liver of fat goose, or of moose (not
    sentimental
perhaps but the urine of purple flowers). I was expecting
the Aztec heart of a young boy. Not the dagger that trimmed it

but the heart itself. But no: I am a hole in the head of the
    Unknown
Soldier; I am the salt of the earth applied to his wound.
I am the lupine in the vase under the mounted moose's head.
    I am

the shy recipient of a single valentine. And I
am a living mock-up of the heart—don't I know its variations?
   The wound
from which the red ink sweetly flows.

Sentience

"The female genital, like the blank page anticipating the poem,
is an absence, a not me, which I occupy.
By occupying absence, I experience myself becoming more
than what I was. The blank page and this genital
are an appeal to being. By being where I was not,
I am no longer self-contained: I experience myself
in the dimensions, contours, textures of my mate.
When she is naked like lava undressed of pine
I not only feel her but see her. She is wrinkled.
I am poor; I will take even the wrinkled.
High country, faceless, rough on the feet, swindling the lungs.
I am poor but igneous landscape asks nothing of me
nor gives me anything I want but myself."

(*Half derived from a student's essay.*)

Wearing White

The old dogged ways of writing poems
cover with snow. Juncos, bodied like lynx tails,
fly out of the empty prison.

Dipping his hand in blood the taxidermist complains
nothing will stay on this white. He raises
a frozen wasp by a leg, beginning to move.

On maples the sensory tips say: we refuse,
not another experiment. They wonder if they are not
warped by feeling. Frosting the interior

that faces them a pocket watch hangs, stopped
and silver. It listens as the leaves clatter
into glassy cornerings. An idea

of what to do with an idea: I am wearing white—
the height of the heart of a tree in my boreal
cloths. My seamstress sets down

her needle, with a headache. Like windows
painted shut, snow everywhere hardens. My hands
are cold, and they must keep cold, like milk.

The Gun Is Such a Horse

The gun is such a horse
people are thrown around by it
it eats carrots and sugarcane
it has an iron shoe for defense and games

The horse though has such
curves if it were a gun
it would shoot itself
its owner would run crying
far into the field

The gun is such a mosquito
thin for any target

But if the mosquito were a gun
earth would be much the same
too much the same

The gun is like the whale
only the whale is blue
and very happy
and suckles her young

The gun must be kept dry of milk
clean of grass
but the mosquito may sit on its barrel
watching and thin

Solvents

Mother used to nest some clothes in a tub of gasoline.
She set it under a fig tree far behind the house
to catch shade. See it burn there? Gasoline

under a fig tree wrote some history once. Gentiles
like she is believe it for its miracles; distant in time
they give her a sign not a sign of the times.

Do not sully her clothes with water!—it's been walked all over.
Drag the foot of a match. The old clothes call for kindling,
naval blues for drowning, pray the family rise

again. Stars should have such a past, a homely
fruit tree for protection. Instead, most universe feels
unthrown shade. Well, let these rags clean (charred

they'd not be clean) while an Israeli widow beats
a burning body with a stick. Yours, enemy. She was once
this laundress stirring fashion with a wand.

Centerfold Reflected in a Jet Window

There is someone naked flying alongside the airplane.
The man in the seat in front of me is trying to hold her.
But she reflects, she is below zero, would freeze the skin
off his tongue.

Beside me also someone is flying.
And I don't say, "Put on your sweater."
And I don't say, "Come back in this minute,"
though she is my daughter.

And there is an old woman riding inside the earth.
Metal shoulders wear her dresses.
She believed she would be an old woman flying alongside
        heaven
because she loved, because she had always loved.

The Mouse

Two have frozen; one—a misfortune—
broke its back; two more ate poison
too soon to reach safety in the live trap;
three were let out in soft yellow weeds.

Bulldozers came. And now this nineteenth
mouse shakes and drums its rhubarb-
spider feet and backs away.
I give it goat cheese and anise cake

to have good memories. "The dark mice
of my past," says Vittorini,
"overran me." And he boarded the long train
to the island of his mother.

Mother's island was a chair, mother's island
was silence inside the plasmic sound
of a mouse. Mother's island had hibiscus,
orange, palm, it was a beautiful place.

And the small meats of their bodies ate seeds—
but not enough so there was any vacant
patch of ground. Up through the space of fear
grew wheat, comb-honey, sunflowers, oaks.

And like the mouse she showed great courage
when she entered the hospital to die
then didn't die and even began to eat.
She thought of heaven, and other scenic places . . .

Now she comes home. The earth is strung and tied
with cold-faded grass. Squirrels flock
and smarten in the short sunlight.
The owl appears by day. She fears forgetting.

Senility

We cannot remember any fatigue of beautiful things, bee songs
in the hives, the gray path-end atop hard Mt. Whitney, the
steady Indians stopping in our kitchens while a corpse
creaked in their dray.
We forget the sweat soaking our view of the borax caravans,
perspiration on our shell at a husband's burial, the stained
gussets of tiny dresses
from when people, of neglect, did not grow so high and the
grandfather of rats walked us thin by eating our grain and
our saddles.

Tell us your name again.

But those things are what we remember best perhaps because
nothing that happens at Bea's Sanitarium rushes to replace
them.
We may have given you your names, but these days they tell
us our hummingbirds that died this fall were really colum-
bine, and the bluejay faithful to the apple tree
was a piece of sky. What is your name again? God knows how
we remember Bea's, except in some way we belong to Bea,
are not your mothers any more.

Never forget whose child you are.

We remember the time, plowing, we found the children of the
earthquake: minds had been planted in our farm, mem-
ories had refused

and only let the hay grow tall. And whose children were they?
    And why didn't their names survive?
They belonged to the sunset flowers and the morning shadow
    of the mountain, free of eternal questions. But you, dearie,
    what was your name?—

            you are the person suffering with the answers.

Open Casket

To see the anemones, urchins, and crabs
take the Pacific Grove
glass-bottomed boat.
The colors are extraordinary
for the glass rejects the surface
of crumpled brine
and substitutes a clear view of
each thing's design
in water-oiled harmony
of movement and pigment.

    So much cooler
    than riding the bus
    between Santa Barbara and San Jose,
    the poor leaving the rich
    to go back where we belong.
    Leaving and entering towns
    by undersized roads,
    passing through dark bean fields
    worked below the hard dust
    of hills, subsisting on coffee
    cream, we read the depot literature
    of miraculous healing,
    in the night heat only a jeweler's window
    filled with amethysts
    frosts over.

    Or San Jose to Sacramento,
    reading the Gospel of John

in a little red pocket version,
going to slide along the floors
of the gold and white capitol,
all the state's children gathered under one roof
and made to think of poppies and mountains.
Certainly too many people—
each someday living
beyond another, being
ready to write a book like John's
to the friend who comes back.

White salts and rusts and mires
where the rivers used to be . . .

Thin wildflowers
and our colored pencils in the grass . . .

But in Monterey Bay,
in the brine the sun has turned
gray, blue, and green at once
like the window of a Greyhound bus,
there's a way to see down in.
How close the slightly unreal colors come,
the spines' red-violet and the blue-black
of shells. It is summer and
vacation there.

for EWM d. 1956

Orange Peels

Orange peels in her skillet like lions in the dark
blackened, witching an aroma through the ancient rooms.
She'd always liked their essence—
said the woman alone in the north of Maine.

It felt like when you were still alive, her preference
to breathe the fruit but not to eat,
her wild hair like foxtails on the freeway shoulders
magnifying the last light.

I had thought she was candying as I liked to do
when there used to be so much time, the hot moon
in a red haze and the crystals cutting through
if only for the hand to touch—

for BJM 1888–1976

The Compound Eye

Shiny beings come down out of the sky
and delve at its eyes so it is blinded
   to see how they fly harp on wedge-shaped harp
into its wound. We do not know
   the origin of the wound.
   A mother bear was seen, a wolf once.
We do not know if it was sickness or a brawl.
               And it cannot see us.

Its mask swings flat against their midst,
its ring-tail sinks too slowly to crush any there.
   The raccoon's mouth stays shut.
Yesterday we couldn't stop watching
   the jumbo emerald and ebony
   dragonflies like glass ferns,
one rhythmical, one pinned and thrumming its crisp
              free wing in bursts—

because we said they were mating.
I went after lunch to see how they lasted.
   The eye-heavy face
of the pedestal, the male, lay as a single
   carpentered shell in the grass.
   Don't you doubt for a minute
that they *had* made love. Higher up
           perhaps. So had the fishflies

we swam in. Torsos and wings
thick and pink as water knotweed

were suspended as if on glass shelves
and kept soaking like orchids or organs.
　　They were moving downshore,
　　　a whole dispensary
of parts that had once clung itchily to any
　　　　　　　　red fisherman's face.

So today, as we winnow the chevron-marked wings from its
　　　gaze,
we think we're used to their intimacy
　　and still we're hypnotized
by so much z-emphatic song: for none of us can tell
　　if at the burial
　　we bury any of the flies
that thousands of times see the same defeat we see
　　　　　　　with their own wondrous eyes.

January Apples

One of the fears I was familiar with was terror of remaining. Remaining, going home, sending off, well-wishing. And so I wrote many letters, took many trips to the mailbox, a short distance. I found, in my path, even closer, an apple tree hosting a huge number of fruits, dropping masses of them, round things into a larger circle on the earth. They were firm, they changed texture. They were yellow, they became purple and cold and chained by snow.

They are floating on a wave
a froth on winter
thrown down and picked up
like the middle of life

And they have been crushed
across the dawn
smeared over the light
like language reserved for windows

Like their red snow
truth decomposes
and new truths land in uniform
shiny shoes whole-hearted

No one will eat them
No one count
them to the last lamb into a crate

January sweetens the mud
opens the tree house
waiting
like seeds and branches
to be secret again

You see
their perfume smoke
their dizziness carry on
until this morning
wholly tender
they are almost gone

but remaining . . . like an ellipse, shape in the haunches of the apples, I remained, heel on their venom. They didn't amuse me, and for that I have to pay in mockery, giddiness, good nature—letting them tempt me.

Letter After the Poems of a Friend

The rat came close, caught our scent
(as if he needed to gazing straight at us)
and ran for water. He moved fast,
while there were still rings in the pond
he was crossing the isthmus.
Reaching, you pulled a drenched white flower
out of the dark.

        That dark,
    the water the berries hung down into,
    a few sweet and warm,
    purple hands, the spring raising water,
    in backyards under thick crabapples
    children tumbling like fruit . . .

One day I had no flowers but we wanted one.
At a round table, devoted to stories, we
set white goat cheese beside the beer, the vase.

I had to, out of the neighbor's garden,
as if from between the teeth of a rat,
steal another rose.

for Lee

Studies in the Imaginary

I

Breakfast for hundreds of believers
is opening morning with devotions.
Willing to think the inexperienced dawn light
    babied me,
I used to sit by a hyacinth—
(some grotto)—and pray in the breath
of its distracting perfume.

To pray was like living on the road
that goes on to someone else's house
even when it is too far to walk.
Now I'm too far away from hometown streets
to know any listener, being among strangers
    approaches
being among the imaginary.

2

The river is a thread, the end licked
to pass through town after town.
To ancestors approaching from the ocean
this land looked just what they had hoped for.
Where they set foot they knew neither the plants
nor animals nor what kind of people.

Their German Bluebird was gold after all.
But they kept on naming. They named a nation
for its feet, its stomach, the back
of its head. But the people,
who already knew about themselves,
called the newcomers murder mysteries.

3

It is a fine day for a strange place.
I've taken a room above a bird's nest.
It is above a pleading noise.
There are more nests higher up.
What all these voices want becomes an ingredient
in a gourmet soup I've never had.

The room's decor equals all the roomers
escaping to separate steamy baths, a nylon
of mist over each face in a mirror
like a teller's window. "Pea soup"
they say of fog, who within their journeys
were straining to see the moment ahead.

4

The sheets are overlaundered and salesmen
rub their elbows raw.
Outside the pane the outdoor bed:
fern shoots over the old fronds, mosquitoes
after blue hairstreaks, smallnesses
runners or laughers could consume.

Violets and lilacs narrowly missing
each other's season.
They don't give in to coincidences or mindread.
They lean on one another and divine
room for the blossom, for the chrysalis' door,
for the wakers.

5

A botany class comes close
where I am wandering the spongy ground around
a spring. How unlikely they will identify me,
stop and pronounce the existence of anyone
moving faster than locust or colt's foot.
But then, if I could even approach, on foot

or with an extrovert word,
I wouldn't bow out to meditate, awkward
as that duck, green and bronze, strolling grass-
        spattered
through bamboo. Strangers
are so fast, no slowing you, no halting the wings
of the hummingbird.

6

There are no longer single rooms:
any bedroom has an unused bed
beside my rumpled one.
I sleep as if beside a corrective mirror
which relieves the maid—
while grassflowers and mosquitoes

crop up, break in, and harry her
on my side of the mirror.
Finally I place you in the pane
you come through like a dove
and the dove's echo from towns I've just
passed through: me suggesting you.

7

Say I know you shallowly, I know you like
a firefly following a plane, no better.
Say it's too early spring for fireflies.
Say I see you planing on the tennis court,
running off your fat, drumming out your sweat,
the art of your oil and water

like two kinds of painting.
Say I paint you sitting outside full courts
with your one white glove on
as it gets dark and you leave.
It all seems so familiar, the dark,
you'd think somebody would be.

8

Your face once lay on mimeograph purple
as you fell to dreaming against the only
printing your work had had. I read your words—
and was happy they were you
but you were also that extended body
that didn't wake up a word.

As for words, this town speaks in a dialect
of mass bells, fire sirens, wind warnings.
Which is which and what should I do?
Go to the center of the room, kneel
at a pew, protect my skin.
But I read your words and am happy they are you.

9

These are the people I have known: the precautious
ferris-wheel operator, the masseur disinfecting
his metal house with carpet broom,
the rootbound man carved from a fern tree,
the wooden boy saint
with lotioned hands behind his back.

But that sailor, that sailor was unreal.
He found someone for everybody.
He gently shouldered two of everything onto his boat,
mating dragonflies of analagous colors
that neither sting nor bite.
He started the world over with deuces.

10

Dear, I pray you think of me, not as a tourist,
but as an enormous melancholy salesman
opening the window and leaning out
where you are in springtime—
so that all the samples fall out of my pockets
into nests and forsythia bushes.

For now I have nothing to show you.
Now I turn back into the cell and find a face
the face of a clock. And a voice the voice of
a cricket. And me suggesting you as one dove
        suggesting
another in another town
believes in the empty air.

Ohio 1975

The Bittern

Because I have turned my head for years
in order to see the bittern
I won't mind not finding
what I am looking for
as long as I know it could be there,
the cover is right,
it would be natural.

I loved you for what you had seen
and because you took me to see things,

alpine flowers
and your heart under your shirt.

The birds that mate for life
we supposed to be happiest,

my green-eyed,
bitter evergreen.

The bough flies back into the night.

I might be driving by a marsh
and suddenly turn my head—
That's not exactly the way you see them, you say.
So I look from the corners of my eyes
as if cheating in school
or overcoming a shyness.

In the end I see
           nothing
but how I go blindly on loving
a life from which something is missing.

Clouds rushing across the sun,
gold blowing down on the reeds—

nothings like these . . .

Sandra McPherson is the author of *Elegies for the Hot Season* and *Radiation*. *The Year of Our Birth* is her third collection. She taught for two years in the University of Iowa Writers' Workshop, and has received an Ingram Merrill Foundation award, a National Endowment for the Arts grant, and a Guggenheim Foundation fellowship. She lives in Portland, Oregon.